Last House on the Block originally published in 2023 by Bassetthound Press, *Targeted Ads* originally published in 2023 in 2023 by BRUISER MAG, *What if Ad Nauseum* originally published in 2024 by Smacked Zine. Cover art by @jas_hice.

ISBN 979-8-9897701-4-4

Published by Hidden Hand Press
www.hiddenhandbooks.com

HIDDEN HAND PRESS

Year of the Rabbit

Poems by Lin Elizabeth

CONTENTS

"...too many serious wounds are carelessly written off as "nothing but shyness"- more often a compliment is stuttered around about because it sets up an automatic and unpleasant dialogue in the woman's mind."

-Clarissa Pinkola Estés,
(Women Who Run With the Wolves)

For Philip.
Feral always in your truth, I'll leave a light on and food by the door.

ON YOUR LAP

"Top has sprung a leak, and the animals that are trapped have all become my pets."

-Kurt Cobain

Funny how humans do not necessarily have a fear of fire,
There must be no fear in our own inventions.
      A bustling baby must be taught that, fire is unsafe
      To not be touched — holy, god-wielding.
      shielding to a light.

I wonder what that process is like, leading a baby's hand to an open flame — to incite fear, as a defense mechanism.

There are beetles that survive in the Northwestern California fires, they mate in the ashes – they find themselves doing dances in the remains.
Friday they nestle in, amongst the dead foliage,
Encouraged to bring some good of it.
Sunday dances after a weekend engulfed in flame.

I want to be Sunday Morning.
      Sunday Morning is on fire,   but smoldering.
      Sunday Morning — is March transition into spring.

There's no innate fear — you and I are just children
watching lights dance, flicker in our eyes.
curled up, marshmallows at the end of our sticks.
like two barn kittens, calicoed you, milky orange for me.

TRANSVERSE ORIENTATION

Moths with wings open, needing to feed.
Transverse orientation enamored with
Freeway lamps.
Non-smokers porches —
The rhythmic thump of
An imposter moon.

Performance is, on occasion, survival.
The rabbit is symbolic of fertility — youth.
A demand of one's body to absolute itself to another's.
Sometimes the crib is creaky,
The bones inside,
too.

The causation of suffering is constant resistance —
Unwillingness to grow and be grown
Soft, you linger here, curious.

There is no suffering to be found when you look in between
the cracks,
only.

The wrinkled light in the distance
The soft quiet in the between,
The prisms the stained glass leaves on your shadows.
Sometimes, I count your
floorboards.

Knowing my dog eyes will always look
at the master before speaking.
How comfortable, it becomes, after —
curl up on your lawn, talking to them damn weeds,
telling them I would kiss their
chlorophylled knees if they had
any.

Dinner Party Affirmations

No grease at these. It'll only cause a headache.
Do not answer things you are uncomfortable with.
Dress to aerate the room. You are a perfume.
Tuck your neck down.
Point your toes inward, resemble the bouquet
in the middle of the table, bones exposed, stems
naked.

Do you see yourself
Remembering your power?

You are allowed to have feral girl table manners,
elbows sloppy on oak wood, edges of your mouth pooling
with crumbs.
saving some for birds after.
If you so choose, slide
out from the entrapment of the equine
dinner table; push away, with
raucous intentions, tense tendons
flex your heel, barely skimming
the hem of the dress on the legs of the
hushed table.
A fast, fine, focal point motion.

Forfeit the serving games, kick an orange from plate to plate,
bite the hand the offers you lamb, refuse to
deserve someone else's sacrifice. No damaged goods.
You are after the right size, right words, right slights of hands
prize, golden goose. Do not become the beveled discarded
dresser on the street up to the
marbled estate; awaiting on a new
owner that will discard it eventually
the same way.
The stuffed rabbit in the room had teeth and claws,
for the same reason
you do.

VULPES

*somewhere in a meadow, seen through a window — there is a rabbit
and there is a fox. Animal instinct is to kill.*
  'How do you make death beautiful, so as not to be haunted by it?'

The blood in the fox's fur never really rinses clean unless the
flow is fast enough;
Still, the fox tries quietly in a stream.
tries to take the evidence of itself, the pack,
Tries to eviscerate its existence in the kingdom of predators.
Its briard fur, its hard nails, teeth, arching back, its bones
which are also the rabbits'.

A child will pick them up; a mother will *hmm* at the cherub,
wash it carefully, like you would around an open gash in the
leg.

      Dominance is to be seen as an open wound.

VULPES, ANOTHER OBSERVATION

I.
Bring her dressings, and alcohol swabs to disinfect
what is marred over, and glistening tongs, in the fluorescence.
Apparatus clean, not the slightest tremor in her paw.
She'll do a reverse husband stitch on your mother —
To loosen the Oedipal grip.

To know the difference between a scalpel and a mini scraper is
to see the curvature, size of the blade.
Each thing has its own intended use and purpose. To choose
to stray is a
choice in its own right.

II.
Dying rabbits sound like screaming mice —They are not quiet
pets.
They are much meaner than you'd suspect, if handled
incorrectly.
A child, who will be pacified, waves to the fox, lunch in her
hair, as usual.
Back to watching the meadow, daisies lurking somehow
means death.

The fox and the rabbit doing Darwin's inevitable dance.
Their ghosts will play after,
They find each other again.

III.
The child will wear raccoon hats, the mother will insist
that the child will grow out of it, eventually, the mother will
have to be dressed, her oranges peeled for her in the morning.
Later, she is much older, like the child she will
pacified, when the sun goes down, the time will confuse her,
the lunch that will end up in her hair, the way the child says
her name, so confidently, so reassured, *mother*, like the child
has known her
for her whole life.

To The Fisherman

Tender in the way that if you press into a sick part
Of the body, it'll respond in a small alarming way.

I've never broken a bone; that surprises people.
I never understood why.
The show it gets; its own cast and dressing.

Is it a right of passage to break something that defines you?
Do baby birds who break their wings cry to their mothers?
Are they chided for the act of falling out of the tree?

I just say: *There are too many pearls on this necklace.*
You think the fisherman would fancy one?

Have you thought about this too?
Mysticism, mother birds, mussels,
Mermaids, the sought after whale.

Ahab, you become —
Lost a leg due to sea madness, they tell you.
Incurable, they tell you.

Look at the ballerina twirl in the music box.
My best harpoon, twined in gold wire.

Whales sleep vertically in the water.
You
      just
           have
                to
                aim down.

TARGETED ADS

My body.
Is not
Allowed to
Talk about
Mirror games.
Dismantle the
Flood gates.

Familiar with.
Breaking dishes.
Pleated hair.
Saying no
Is congruent
With saying
Yes, Poet.

Can I
Insist that
You're here
With me?
Gently, now.

I plead
"I would
Like to
Look like
My second
Grade picture,
Again, please."

Clench, release.
Guided meditation.
"Savior, Take
My hand
Make it clean
Without asking
About harm done."

Am I
Allowed to
Say her
Name and
Swallow it.

GIRL ANIMA

Sometimes, I believe in   roadkill;
The idea that a death   happens
By the trial and error of   movement.

Grief is a thread, we   animals
Try to eye a needle,   thumbless.
It's as if you are   plagued.

To call a bird by its   genus
Is to call it by its   God's
Name. Class follows all   Orders

In kingdom that the   moon
Has decided to rule.   species
Of the damned: do the   opposite.

Suggest the headline read   *deer*
killed by gun, instead of   children,
Birthday attendees, gas clerks,   daughters,

Nightclub goers, those who are   Sacred
grocery store goers, people of full   life;
Their bags full of oranges to be   consumed.

KITTEN OBSERVATIONS

Even perceivably domesticated mammals want
authenticity. The salmon salt licked off the plastic you
unwrap, googling later if hickory is dangerous for cats.
Their only interest is in your sacred feather boa– the noisy
rolling cylindrical ball, seasick blue tuffs – palm sized lion
stalks prey mouth agape growling at any detected movement – even at
kill site.

Something

is

calling

me

by
    The nape of my   Neck.

Perched in the tree you dress, delicately in December.
Ready to give in to every instinct; exhalation.
Leap from the bed to the bricklayer mantle, gravity has no
hold on your vertebrae.

13

To depart from the wild,
can do unsuspecting
damage to those
unfamiliar that there was
a choice.

Keeping Un-blood brothers apart is notoriously hard.

Run the faucet,   keep it there.

The pretend heavy yellow box must be in front of the barrier.
They won't have fun   playing amongst themselves.

The begging for forgiveness, oh god, the allowance of it.
As a slow   blink of *yes.*

Permission is a gratitude; sometimes you stand in front of
your grandmother's in-home green oxygen tank. Feel with
your small hands the oxygen she breathes, outside
encapsulated, quietly, you decide to move.

Distraction is key.
Some quiet power of stillness.

Something like a hunt, an oasis, a sunbeam on the hardwood.

---

*I want them back, the teeth they lost, the whiskers dropped on the
hardwood, width permission granted, I want to store them until they
tell me the sorcery of growing old. The slow blink is a butterfly kiss
from a creature that would snack on your dead body, if left to that.
The love earned is worth it; I read somewhere that the frequency of*

the purr of a kitten is known to be similar to to a heart beat of a
babies; the kitten bonds in much the same way a child does to it's
perceived caretakers,
The human want to be accepted is challenged by the cat.
Maslow's predator.

Adoptee me.

105 Main Street, Redacted Place, 95646

How relieved she must
Have been, playing God
A full can, not dead.

Overlooked by guilt,
Rather sprung to life in a
Pool hall, its green lights.

Poetic, even when
Unsealing itself dimly
To return foothilled.

SUMMER SONG

Feet hung out the window,
arches swallowed in the lick
of a valley mirage of humidity.
Cotton was picked in this heat.
Should've been out of my mouth;
the kiss of creek mouth will always
be sweeter than the one
on the rockshore. Unsure of
onlookers, voyeurs of wishing stones
the energy found in tidepools,
creatures that absorb its water,
exiles of the ocean. Make me a home, too
soak the sun. balance the ball of it on
my head. See how well I adapt.

LAST HOUSE ON THE BLOCK

Guttural in the sound
The way the 'O' fills it up. The air. The air..
Singing out the harsh fatality of ending a word. Almost too
large in the mouth.
Dog eat dog eat dog eat dog — eat.
Teeth garnished with soot.
Stray dogs on this side of the street do not, can not,
Understand what 'stay' means. Untaught manners.
Scrappy tableside habits, teeth gnawing at cedar legs.
They tell me, chant.
Go somewhere, do not come back until
There is your blood in your matted fur.
Your teeth are too clean to stay.
The snow, woe of it. sewing the patches of hope
For the white winter. The oak cloaked in the yard.
Lonesome again, there's that 'o' sound but
not long, like in god, song, mom, pond, psalms, my dawns.
Mimicking the way I've calmed stray dogs
in their militia of being.

"O there you are, O! Foxhound,
Safe and sound, the moon alabaster round.
Howling at the camino's rust colored smoke sound,
Familiar, alley tomcats, Screaming, spellbound.
Smoke signals, it blows halfway 'round the block,
Takes a few seconds, I reckon."

NEIGHBOR

Neighbor, your outdoor garden is March and April and
May in the middle of February. Neighbor, I've learned from
you to slowly make my bed.
Neighbor, on the inhale you remind me to say my name.
Neighbor, I've had panic attacks in your presence.
Neighbor, on the exhale you remind me to say my name.
Neighbor, it was too long ago to remember why.
Neighbor, I've noticed you've been eating again.
Neighbor, it's an act of god, a god kinder than thought.
Neighbor, do you hear the bells?
Neighbor, the light won't go out
Neighbor, all the shoes are done dropping.
Neighbor, I understand why you have dogs — the protection
they keep.
Neighbor, I prayed for this for you.
Neighbor, I only wish for oil lamp talks.
Neighbor, I think you look too much like my mother from an
angle.
Neighbor, but then you speak and I am free.

WHAT IF AD NAUSEAM

What if you go on a **w**   **a**   **l**   **k**   today?
What if the sallow dog on the corner is someone else's?
What if the dog on the corner bites you?
What if the bite is so bad, you must go to the hospital?
What if the doctors wheel you to a room unable to escape?
What if in the hospital, you are roomed with a dying man?
What if the dying man owned the dog?
What if the man whose dog bit you, knew that his dog bit
you?
What if he knew he was dying also?

      What would you   kindly   ask   of   me?

                    A   stranger

        Once bitten   but   marred
        to almost execution.

    Do you think he'll still forgive me?

The dog, I mean.

        bad dog
        bites stranger
        death sometimes bites

the ones who are alone
unwillingly.

What if he doesn't forgive me?
What if I have a dog haunter?
What if he's one of those bees that stay alive after stinging?
I believe I may be haunted by a dog.
Dog of grief. Dog of burden. My good dog days.
Dog of proof. Dogged heart. Dog eyes. Dog eared
reminders about being good — of value.

EAST TO WEST

Tell me again, how my body is a machine.
How it's a clock: a working
Living, hovering, suffering thing.

Tell me again, how it's intrinsic, built,
The desire and suffering of desire,
Tell me again how
        it won't stop, *beautifully.*

This life,
        This *body*,
The way time moves,
        Unless I will it to stop.

Remind me how it's beautiful,
Bring your arrival to me, like a cat dropping
A mouse. Solve it. Tell me about the relief.
Trace it into the back of my corneas.

Salmon from the
        West coast tastes fresher,
But
I wonder if they can feel
        danger in the water,
like I can.

Always have. Ears perked at
The slightest movement.

to be on haunches at all times.

AN APOLOGY TO A STRAY

Now listen,
We've both scoured through trash
To find something to dine on.
We are both creatures of instinct
Habit-to-destruction, alas until finding God.
You exhale exit the idea of stray, misplaced, unkind,
Unloved, both the dog and —

I've done the dogged days, sleeping
Outside God's house, knocking with
Blood knuckles for something to
Inhale life back into me.

I've sat on the porch, and howled,
Wondering why the moon disappears
Always on my loneliest nights.

May I play again, without consequence –
Child twirling, a fairy headband in her hair,
The strands flying as she spins,

I want to play your game of fetch, retrieve,
Remind myself, the belonging.
I belong, so long as I find joy in it.

ACKNOWLEDGEMENTS

I would like to thank the reader, their time, span of attention and space. I would like to thank my beautiful community of writers in my area (and elsewhere! Of course, elsewhere!) that prove time and again that poetry is still alive. The cover artist, Jas Hice, who has always been a great artist and an even more valuable supporter and dear friend has been vastly appreciated in more ways than just one. I would like to thank my editors, those who have helped me guide this book to fruition, those who read side by side with me and helped me see my errors and things through a different perspective. You are all irreplaceable. I would also like to extend my love and appreciation to everyone who's held space for me in places. Your grace, shared experiences, humor, and gratitude beyond measure fills my pores and makes me sweeter. For that, I thank you a million times.

And, Tony, my font picker, my test dummy on sounds and words, and honestly the smartest human. Thank you. Thank you.

ABOUT THE AUTHOR

Lin Elizabeth (she/her) is a poet residing in Arkansas, working and trying to understand the meaning of grieving. She's written about various topic including sex work, addiction, and trauma awareness. Her poems have debuted in many places, among them are *Smacked! Zine, Tilted House Press, BRUISER magazine, Basset Hound Press, Dream Boy Book Club , Hypertrophic Press, Goat's Milk Magazine* and others.

www.ingramcontent.com/pod-product-compliance
Lightning Source LLC
Chambersburg PA
CBHW020348130626
46549CB00003B/1348